Lincoln & Lady

Cathy A. Woodson
Author

Sarah M. Wessel
Illustrator

gfg ceg msc mrm

This is my friend Abraham. I travel with him a lot. Sometimes I just grab hold of his shoulder and off we go on an adventure. I have even perched on his hat and hid in his beard, so I would get a great view.

"Well, hello there!" he exclaimed one day as he saw me sunning myself on a marigold. He picked me up and settled me on his shoulder.

Abraham and I got to know each other on our walks around his garden. He told me his name was Abraham, but some people called him "Abe." He frowned when he said his nickname. "I like Abraham," I chirped into his ear. "Good," he said. "I will call you Lady."

Ever since then, we have been great friends. He has told me many secrets. I have promised to never tell them to anyone.

Abraham is President of the United States. He has a very important job. One day he got a letter from a man named David Wills. Mr. Wills asked Abraham to come to a town called Gettysburg. I'm not sure where that is.

I asked Abraham who Mr. Wills was. Abraham told me that people were going to be making speeches in Gettysburg. Mr. Wills invited Abraham to stay at his house as there was nowhere else to stay.

Mr. Wills must be a very important man in Gettysburg.

"Lady," asked Abraham. "How would you like to go on a train ride with me? We are going to Gettysburg."

I excitedly squeaked my little chirrup and bounced up and down. I loved adventures with Abraham.

I saw Abraham packing his bags and knew that we would be going away soon.

When it was time to go, Abraham put out his hand, and I hopped on it. Up and up and up he lifted me on to the very top of his hat. Abraham is very tall. No one would see me up there.

We took a special train to Gettysburg. The wheels went clickety clack, clickety clack. Riding a train was great fun!

As we were riding along, Abraham took a paper out of his pocket and began to study it. He would glance out the window and then back at his paper. I peeked over his shoulder and wished I could read.

I chirruped in his ear,
and he gave a little grin
while he worked.

We finally arrived at Gettysburg. There was a group of men who greeted us at the train station. Abraham shook everyone's hand. Mr. Wills led the way to his house. It was November and the weather was very chilly.

We walked a block up the street to Mr. Wills' house. I sat on Abraham's hat and looked all around me.

I thought I saw a cannonball lodged into the side of Mr. Wills' house.

That evening we had supper with David Wills and a group of men I didn't know. I think they were very important people. I just stayed out of sight and listened.

Later, there was a crowd gathered outside Mr. Wills' house. They wanted to see Abraham. They wanted him to speak to them. Abraham waved and said a few words. I think Abraham was tired.

It was getting late and tomorrow was a big day. Abraham said goodnight to his hosts and grabbing his hat where I was sitting, headed up the stairs to bed.

It was late in the night, and Abraham still worked on his piece of paper. Finally, he put it away and blew out the lamp. I snuggled next to his ear and hummed softly. "Thanks Lady," he said. Soon I heard him snoring.

After breakfast, Abraham lifted me onto his hat and we got onto a horse that seemed little because Abraham was so tall. It was too chilly out to ride on his hat, so I crawled into his beard to keep warm. I poked my little head out every now and again to see the sights.

We saw fields and more fields. They looked like they had been hurt. There were ruts everywhere.

"Why are we looking at the fields?" I asked Abraham. He turned to the other men who were riding along with us. "So, this is where our brave men fought?" he asked.

Abraham was very thoughtful. He would hear my question and talked to the other men answering my question at the same time. I just had to pay attention.

Later that day, we went to a field that was going to be a graveyard. I thought this was a strange place to meet. I whispered in Abraham's ear, "Why are we here?"

Abraham looked down at the paper in his hand. I think it was a program of the day's events. He whispered back to me, "We are going to talk about the soldiers who fought here. They died for our country, Lady. It's the right thing to do."

I snuggled into Abraham's beard out of the cold. A man named Mr. Everett was introduced to the crowd. Mr. Everett was the main speaker, because no one knew if Abraham could make the journey. Mr. Everett talked for a long time. I was getting sleepy.

Then it was Abraham's turn to talk. He only spoke for a few minutes and then he sat down. I don't think the crowd realized he had finished speaking. After a few moments, they clapped loudly.

After the speeches, we headed back to Mr. Wills' house for lunch. I stayed in Abraham's beard where I would be safe.

An older man named John Burns came to chat with Abraham. They decided to go to a church that afternoon. The men talked about the battle that had taken place in the little town. Mr. Burns was very proud that he helped protect his hometown.

Abraham was ready to take the train back to Washington. He reached up and gently touched his beard. "Just making sure you are there, Lady," he said. "Let's go home to Tad."

Tad was Abraham's son. He wasn't feeling well, and Abraham was anxious to get home, too.

I climbed out of Abraham's beard and settled on his shoulder right next to his ear. Very softly, I started to hum a tune I had heard earlier that day. It was called "The Battle Hymn of the Republic." (Mine eyes have seen the glory...)

I could see Abraham begin to relax. He smiled as he said, "That's the ticket, Lady." Slowly his eyes closed as I continued to hum to him.

It turned out that Abraham wasn't feeling well either. After our visit to Gettysburg, he was ill for almost three weeks. While he was ill, he read me letters that he received about his speech.

Now, Abraham's speech is very well known. Everyone knows it as "Lincoln's Gettysburg Address." And I was there with my friend.

Hi, I'm Lady.
I'm a little lady bug.

My feet are very sticky.
Sticky feet help me to climb
and hang on to trees and
branches. I have used
my sticky feet to go on
many adventures.